BUILDING
BOARD
DIVERSITY

Jennifer M. Rutledge

NATIONAL
CENTER FOR
NONPROFIT
BOARDS

**NATIONAL
CENTER FOR
NONPROFIT
BOARDS**

Suite 510
2000 L Street, NW
Washington, DC
20036-4907

Tel. 202-452-6262
Fax 202-452-6299

The mission of the National Center for Nonprofit Boards is to improve the effectiveness of the more than one million nonprofit organizations throughout the United States by strengthening their boards of directors.

To carry out its mission, NCNB provides several programs and services to board members, chief executives, and other nonprofit leaders. Specifically, NCNB:

■ Publishes booklets and other material related to nonprofit boards. Nonprofit leaders have purchased more than 250,000 copies of these books, booklets, audiotapes, and videotapes, making NCNB the world's largest publisher of material on nonprofit governance.

■ Organizes workshops, conferences, and other meetings, including a workshop series, an annual National Leadership Forum, and more than 100 tailored board development programs each year.

■ Provides information and advice to thousands of nonprofit leaders, journalists, educators, and others who call the Board Information Center each year.

Established in 1988 by Independent Sector and the Association of Governing Boards of Universities and Colleges, the National Center for Nonprofit Boards is a 501(c)(3) nonprofit organization.

NCNB received a lead grant from the W.K. Kellogg Foundation and continues to receive grants from corporations, foundations, and individuals. Income from the sale of publications, fees for meetings and training programs, and membership dues are also important sources of financial support for NCNB and its activities.

The views in each NCNB publication are those of its author, and do not represent official positions of the National Center for Nonprofit Boards or its sponsoring organizations. Please contact NCNB to obtain information about other publications, the nationwide Board Information Center, workshops and conferences, and membership.

**This publication, part of NCNB's Board Diversity Project, was produced
with support from the Ford Foundation.**

Project Director	Maureen K. Robinson
Editor	Ellen Cochran Hirzy
Designer	Douglas Dunbebin, Alphawave Designs
Production Manager	Richard Moyers

B *uilding Board Diversity* is an important part of a project that the National Center for Nonprofit Boards (NCNB) has organized to help nonprofit organizations create and sustain diverse and inclusive boards. Through the project and with the help of many individuals in the nonprofit community, NCNB has been able to gain a deeper understanding of the value of gathering to the organization all the perspectives and experiences needed to do meaningful and effective work.

NCNB gratefully acknowledges the support of the Ford Foundation, particularly Emmett Carson for his interest and support of the Board Diversity Project. Sandra T. Gray, vice president of Independent Sector, chaired the advisory committee, contributing to many aspects of the project her knowledge of the nonprofit sector and her personal commitment to creating a more inclusive nonprofit community. Maureen Robinson, NCNB's director of education, provided oversight for the project with her usual intelligence and competence.

Other advisers included: Etha Henry, United Way of New York City; Anne B. Hoover, Partnership with Youth; Kim Igoe, American Association of Museums; many of NCNB's board development associates; and representatives of allied nonprofit service organizations who read and reacted to information and written materials as they developed.

NCNB recruited two invaluable resources for the project: Jennifer Rutledge, and Giachello and Associates.

As the author of this publication and the developer of related training materials, Jennifer Rutledge brought many years of experience working with diversity issues in the nonprofit and corporate sectors. With her partner in Delphi Consulting Group, Melvin T. Williams, she has built numerous bridges between the theory and the practice of diversity management in the workplace and among volunteers, including boards of directors.

Research activities were organized and conducted by Giachello and Associates. Aida L. Giachello, Mara T. Patermaster and Donna Ruscavage organized and conducted the focus groups, interviews, survey and bibliographic research that is summarized in the appendix. These activities significantly broadened participation in the development of this publication and NCNB's related services.

Last, we gratefully acknowledge the assistance of hundreds of nonprofit leaders who answered questions and shared opinions about diversity in their organizations. Without their willingness to give their time and to be candid about successes and challenges, the Board Diversity Project could not have moved forward.

NANCY R. AXELROD
President
National Center for Nonprofit Boards

Although nonprofit board composition is often the result of serendipity, inertia, and happenstance, *effective* boards rarely result from anything other can careful thought and planning. Boards that are diverse—that reflect the communities they serve—are not accidental accomplishments. A diverse and effective board requires commitment, self-knowledge, and an openness to change. A diverse and effective board is willing to engage in an ongoing process that helps identify prospective board members, keeps members engaged and productive, and helps members to renew their commitment to the organization and its mission.

Notice that we did not say "keeps *minority* board members engaged and productive," or "helps *minority* board members to renew their commitment." Although new members who bring diversity to a board may strongly, and justifiably, resent an organization's failure to acknowledge their potential to contribute to the board beyond mere representation, what NCNB learned as it developed this book was the extent to which *all* board members, not just those members who bring diversity to an organization's volunteer leadership, must feel both welcome and well used if they are to be effective. The first steps in the process outlined in this book involve assessments that will lead to identifying strong board candidates with the backgrounds, characteristics and skills that an organization needs. While much of this publication elaborates on these first deliberate steps that boards must take to become more inclusive and receptive to change, a significant part of *Building Board Diversity* focuses on the kinds of basic board practices that are essential to successful identification, recruitment, and orientation of board members.

The purpose of *Building Board Diversity* is to encourage board and senior staff to look at board composition with clear eyes:

■ to examine the organization's mission, and to consider both the community in which the organization exists and the community it primarily serves;

■ to see what an inclusive board can contribute to an organization's effectiveness and credibility; and

■ to see with similar clarity the full range of abilities and expertise that will be needed from the board, not just the visible signs of "difference."

As with other NCNB publications, we have proposed a process, recommended strategies, and provided tools and other information that will make it easier for an organization to move forward. *Building Board Diversity* is meant to encourage chief executives, board chairs, and the chairs of nominating committees to begin if they haven't already, to reconsider if they have made a false start, and to see building board diversity as a process, not a goal that can be reached and then left behind.

The appendix is an effort to share the research we undertook in order to understand the context for board diversity. It is easy to discuss diversity from the aspect of "what should be." We thought the project would benefit from learning "what is" as well.

There is no formula for building a diverse board. It is not enough to hold a mirror to the demographics of the community or the demographics of the organization's current constituency. The board may need to be the organization's agent for change, reflecting in its composition the strategic goals of the organization, not its current reality. The real question may not be "Who do we serve or represent?" but "Who should we, or must we, serve if we are to accomplish our mission?"

In the best sense, this publication is a work in progress. We welcome your comments, suggestions and criticisms.

*"Diversity is
pluralism and the
acceptance of pluralism
in the larger society."* [1]

Change is inevitable. In a progressive country change is constant. — BENJAMIN DISRAELI

*"Diversity is
achieving racial and
ethnic representation."*

*"Diversity means
building broad-based
relationships with
the community."*

---

[1] These quotes, and others that appear later in this book, are from participants in focus groups that were part of the research component of the Board Diversity Project.

The nation's growing cultural diversity is one of the most highly publicized changes occurring in our society today. Shifting demographics have been an incentive for many nonprofit organizations to examine their policies, practices, organizational culture, and structure to prepare for meeting the challenges and benefiting from the opportunities inherent in a diverse society. Most organizations conclude from this examination that they need to make a stronger commitment to inclusiveness. Leadership for change must occur at many levels in an organization, but the board of directors plays a critical role. As board members welcome diversity and value difference, they stand to make tremendous gains in their vitality and effectiveness, both individually and as a working team.

What Is Diversity?

Simply stated, "diversity" means difference—in race, gender, ethnicity, age, socioeconomic class, religion, sexual orientation, skills and abilities, politics, family structure, and a host of other qualities (see Figure 1). Many organizations begin addressing diversity in terms of visible differences. They choose this starting point partly because there is a long history of discrimination based on visible difference, and laws have been enacted prohibiting discriminatory behavior. In addition, the stereotypes and assumptions that lead to oppression usually are based on visible or unchangeable attributes. Organizations also focus on cultural diversity, defining "culture" as the values, practices, patterns, and customs of a group of people or society.

But people can be different in a variety of ways, some less visible than others. One challenge to those who want to build a diverse board is to reinforce this fact. Another challenge is to avoid assuming that there is a "cookbook" or checklist that board members can use to understand and work effectively with a diverse group of prospective board members. The irony of the "cookbook" approach is that it ignores the very differences that organizations are supposedly trying to embrace when they make a commitment to be more inclusive. By failing to acknowledge the many dimensions of diversity, organizations can also end up perpetuating stereotypes.

The various combinations of differences that can exist within one person present the greatest opportunities. Rather than using an individual's cultural background as the sole defining factor, organizations can find out about everything prospective board members have to offer. On an inclusive board, individual board members contribute an array of talents, skills, and interests

Figure 1
What Is Diversity?

People are different in many ways. Here are some examples:

▲ race

▲ culture

▲ national origin

▲ region

▲ gender

▲ sexual orientation

▲ age

▲ marital status

▲ politics

▲ religion

▲ ethnicity

▲ physical ability

▲ mental ability

▲ family structure

▲ socioeconomic class

▲ values

. . . and the list goes on.

CHAPTER ONE

"Organizations must be aware that when recruiting one Hispanic, this

that result from their own experiences and origins. Collectively, the board is enriched by diversity, as individuals take advantage of their differences to work successfully together on behalf of the organization.

who are part of the organization, keep them involved, and get the most from the relationship. The primary reason for addressing diversity is not just to have a visually diverse board of directors, but to develop a productive group of diverse volunteer leaders.

"Diversity won't work if there's a quota system."

individual is not necessarily representative of all Hispanics. There needs to be greater awareness of diversity within cultures."

Developing a diverse board is a commitment to creating a process and a climate that is inclusive and works for everyone. All individuals are encouraged to make their maximum contribution. All individuals are valued for their perspectives, their talents, their contacts, and their knowledge of the community.

Diversity differs from the familiar concepts of equal employment opportunity (EEO) and affirmative action. EEO is the philosophy and resulting policies that provide a legal framework for inclusiveness on the staff level. Affirmative action is a practice designed to correct historical imbalances in the workplace and ensure that organizations live up to their EEO policies.

An organization's legal obligation to provide equal opportunity in the workplace creates a broad moral obligation for the board to look at its own diversity. Diversity initiatives help boards work effectively with those from diverse backgrounds

Benefits to the Organization

An organization that recognizes the importance of developing a diverse board and the advantages of inclusiveness will realize the following benefits:

■ greater participation and interest from board members, staff, and volunteers within the organization and from allies and advocates outside the organization

■ sound, effective board practices and processes that capitalize on *all* the available talent

■ creativity and innovation because a variety of ideas and viewpoints are welcomed and shared

■ better-informed policy decisions that ultimately strengthen management and improve the organization's ability to fulfill its mission.

Addressing diversity is a process, not a program. Like any successful strategic initiative, building a diverse board requires vision, planning, and leadership. Sensitivity and awareness training may be part of the early phases, but workshops alone will not create an organization that values all board members, encourages the sharing of ideas, and maximizes individual contributions.

Organizations that develop diversity initiatives generally move along a continuum from the first stage of building awareness to the final stage of valuing diversity. Most diversity initiatives will include the following phases:

■ planning
■ building awareness
■ taking action
■ evaluation

In exploring ways to build a diverse board and planning activities toward that goal, organizations have several alternatives. Some steps are essential to the process, some are desirable, and others are optional (figures 2 and 3). A number of factors influence the development of plans and activities, including board and staff commitment, budget considerations, other organizational plans, time, and human resources (both numbers and skill levels).

Commitment, coordination, and communication are critical to the success of a diversity initiative. The board chair and other board leaders must be committed from the outset to finding ways to deal with diversity and to making the initiative work. The board may want to hold informational meetings that acquaint board members with the issues before taking the first steps (see chapter 4). Because building a diverse board is a process, the board should coordinate the effort with the organization's strategic, long-range, and annual plans. Plans that specifically address questions of inclusiveness signal an organization-wide commitment that will bolster a board diversity initiative. The board also should review plans to develop a diverse staff or to establish culturally relevant programs and services so they can assess the potential for coordination. Good internal communication is essential. Keeping board members, key staff, and those with vested interests in the organization informed and soliciting opinions from them will contribute to the success of the initiative.

Who Should Be Involved?

Building a diverse board is the board's responsibility. For practical purposes, much of the planning can be delegated to a task force consisting of the board chair, a small group of board members,

Figure 2
Phases of a Diversity Initiative

and the chief executive or the nominating committee, if appropriate. The board chair's leadership is key. He or she must set the tone for others' involvement by providing strong leadership and making a visible personal commitment.

The task force members' responsibilities can include recommending direction, planning activities, and keeping other board members informed. They can also help evaluate progress and decide steps for follow-up. Task force members should not, however, be the only board members involved. Every board member has a responsibility to secure the organization's future, and building a diverse board is one way to carry out this responsibility.

The chief executive's active participation is also fundamental to the success of the initiative. He or she knows what the organization needs from the board in order to serve its constituency well and what qualities should be sought in new board members. The chief executive usually has well-established, broad-based community relationships and can be a significant help when it comes to identifying and recruiting potential board members.

It is appropriate to involve other stakeholders in the process as it unfolds. For example, the planning phase will be most productive if it includes a combination of board, staff, and people from outside the organization who have an investment in its success (such as community leaders, potential board members, funders, or consultants). Key staff and other board members can be brought into the organizational assessment phase. Outside trainers and consultants can design, conduct, and evaluate training programs. Outside evaluators, board, staff, or any combination of these groups can conduct evaluation. When determining who should be involved, board members should keep in mind what skills potential participants bring to the process, who is willing to commit time and energy, and what the budget considerations are.

Advisory Groups

Many organizations have developed advisory groups and panels to help them address questions of board diversity. These groups can work with the board in every phase of a diversity initiative, from assessing the organization to developing and implementing plans. An effective advisory group can be the long-term link between the organization and the community. It is also an excellent way to involve people who are in high demand and can only devote limited time to the organization.

Figure 3
Phases in Building a Diverse Board

PHASE 1: PLANNING			
ACTIVITIES	**ESSENTIAL**	**DESIRABLE**	**OPTIONAL**
Informational meetings	▲		
Commitment to move forward	▲		
Preliminary organizational assessment	▲		
Framework for plan development	▲		
Chief executive involvement	▲		
Coordination with other organizational plans	▲		
Training programs		▲	
Staff involvement		▲	
Outside consultants		▲	
Community outreach			▲
Advisory groups			▲

PHASE 2: BUILDING AWARENESS			
ACTIVITIES	**ESSENTIAL**	**DESIRABLE**	**OPTIONAL**
Informational meetings	▲		
Written commitment	▲		
Vision, reaffirmation of mission	▲		
Training programs	▲		
Plan development	▲		
Chief executive involvement	▲		
Coordination with other organizational plans	▲		
Staff involvement	▲		
Organizational culture, board functions, and board systems analysis		▲	
Outside consultants		▲	
Community outreach		▲	
Advisory groups		▲	

PHASE 3: TAKING ACTION			
ACTIVITIES	**ESSENTIAL**	**DESIRABLE**	**OPTIONAL**
Informational meetings	▲		
Organizational culture, board functions, and board systems analysis	▲		
Community outreach	▲		
Recruitment activities	▲		
Retention activities	▲		
Progress review and contingency plan development	▲		
Chief executive involvement	▲		
Staff involvement	▲		
Follow-up and reinforcement activities for training		▲	
Team-building activities			▲
Outside consultants			▲

PHASE 4: EVALUATION AND BEYOND			
ACTIVITIES	**ESSENTIAL**	**DESIRABLE**	**OPTIONAL**
Informational meetings	▲		
Plan review and adjustment	▲		
Coordination with other organization plans	▲		
Follow-up and reinforcement activities for training	▲		
Recruitment activities	▲		
Retention activities	▲		
Team-building activities	▲		
Implement changes in board functions and systems	▲		
Changes in organizational culture	▲		
Collaboration and community outreach	▲		
Chief executive involvement	▲		
Staff involvement	▲		
Reaffirmation of commitment to diversity		▲	
Advisory groups		▲	
Outside consultants			▲

Advisory groups can be formal or informal, depending on how involved the group will be in the diversity initiative. Here are some tips on forming and working with advisors:

■ Be clear about your expectations, and be able to articulate them. Do not expect advisory groups to do work that should really be assigned to the board.

■ Help advisory group members understand the level of commitment the board has given the initiative. Make sure that the board chair and chief executive are part of the discussions.

■ Share information with advisory group members about the various stages of the initiative and the status of the process. Keep them informed of progress.

■ Remember that there are differences within cultures, races, and ethnicities. Do not expect one representative to speak for everyone.

Advisory groups can bring added benefits beyond the diversity initiative. They can help expand knowledge of the organization within various communities. Some advisory group members may make excellent candidates for board membership. It is important to remember, however, that advisory groups should not be the only place in which diversity exists in the organization. If the board is really committed to the initiative, diversity must become evident on the board.

Consultants

An outside consultant brings an experienced, objective point of view to the many complex aspects of a diversity initiative. A number of groups and consultants are working with organizations in diversity. In fact, diversity is now considered an industry. When working with a consultant, contract with him or her for the full process, not just for one part. The board often will carry out the final diversity plan and activities after the consultant's contract has ended. (Figure 4 suggests guidelines for choosing a consultant.)

Getting Board Members Interested

Not all board members will be willing and ready to address the complex questions surrounding diversity. Those who try to introduce issues may be resisted and questioned because others feel uncomfortable or perhaps even threatened. Some may ignore potential problems and believe that some issues are best left to resolve themselves. In some boards, there may be opposition because the board never discusses concerns with candor. Board members may also feel that discussing differences is really opening Pandora's box.

Fundamental change in an organization can be challenging to initiate and bring about. An important aspect of leadership for change is helping people face the difficulties they may have with moving from the known to the unknown. Board members who choose to become pioneers of diversity must consider these challenges and adjust the scope and nature of their activities to suit the organizational climate and the board's style of working together. Invest enough time at the beginning of the process to provide information, answer questions, respond to concerns, and invite participation. When board members buy into the importance of inclusiveness at the board level, the process will be smoother and ultimately more effective.

To strengthen board members' confidence and commitment:

■ Use board meetings and board information materials to highlight emerging issues.

■ Identify and seek out board members who are strong allies and advocates, and brainstorm with them on how to present the issues to the entire board.

■ Hold informal discussions led by the board chair on the importance of building a diverse board and developing appropriate plans.

■ Incorporate information on changing demographics and implications for the organization into board retreats and other board development activities.

■ Make board diversity a discussion topic at board orientation sessions.

■ Include board diversity issues in the board's self-assessment process.

Many boards break new ground when they introduce the subject of board diversity. The board's own dynamics, as well as the history and culture of the organization, will affect the way the board launches its initiative. Although approaches may differ, every organization will benefit from careful planning that provides a foundation and a framework for the important discussions that follow. The planning phase has three aspects: (1) assessing organizational readiness, (2) analyzing board composition, needs, and decision-making roles, and (3) developing a plan.

Organizational Readiness

An important first step is to gain some insights into the nature of the diversity issues facing the organization and determine the organization's and the board's readiness to begin building diversity. This information is essential to designing appropriate plans.

Both informal and formal assessment methods, depending on the traditions of the organization, can be effective. Informal assessment can begin with a roundtable discussion by the diversity task force—or another small group of board members—designed to

■ provide information on the impact of changing community bases;

■ discuss current organizational plans developed to meet the needs of the changing community and those the organization serves;

■ determine areas in which the board needs to develop policies and action plans that will move the organization forward in addressing diversity issues; and

■ develop strategies to incorporate the topic in the board's work plan.

The Diversity Issues Discussion Guide (Figure 5) is a useful catalyst for discussion.

Once the task force has met, the entire board can come together to discuss the group's findings. The board should affirm its commitment and create a broad framework (in a written plan) for developing a diverse board.

The board also may use formal assessment methods, such as surveys and questionnaires, if it needs more information or if board members feel that people may find it difficult to share information in an open forum. The questions and issues raised in Figure 5 may serve as the basis for a confidential survey of individual board members' opinions and suggestions.

Figure 5
Diversity Issues Discussion Guide

1. Building a diverse board of directors for this organization means:

2. Developing a diversity initiative is important because this board should be better able to:

   a.

   b.

   c.

   OR

3. I don't think it is important to develop a diversity initiative because:

4. It is important to develop a diversity initiative now because:

   OR

5. It is not important to develop a diversity initiative now because:

6. The most rewarding aspect about being a member of this board is:

7. The most challenging aspect of being a member of this board is:

8. The three most critical issues facing this organization are:

   a.

   b.

   c.

9. The greatest challenge to building a diverse board is:

10. If one thing could be accomplished as a result of a board diversity initiative, it should be:

11. I see the board engaging in the following types of activities to build diversity:

12. I am willing to commit to the following to help make the board's activities successful:

Figure 6
Board Profile Worksheet*

This tool helps to identify current gaps and desired characteristics on your board at this stage in your nonprofit's life. Whether this tool is reviewed by a single individual or at a nominating committee meeting, mark the grid for each characteristic that is currently filled by one or more board members. After that, you can more easily identify gaps that need to be filled. Please note that each number represents the name of a current board member. Each letter represents the name of a prospective board member.

CATEGORIES TO CONSIDER	CURRENT BOARD MEMBERS (199_)				PROSPECTIVE BOARD MEMBERS (199_–_)			
Area of expertise/ professional skills:	1	2	3	4	A	B	C	D
Organizational and financial management								
Special program focus of our nonprofit (e.g. education, health, public policy, etc.)								
Administration								
Business/corporate								
Finance ▲ *Accounting*								
▲ *Banking and trusts*								
▲ *Investments*								
Fund raising (both professional fund raisers and those with leverage in getting funds)								
Government regulations								
Government representative								
Law								
Marketing								
Personnel								
Physical plant (architect, engineer)								
Strategic or long-range planning								
Public relations								
Real estate								
Representative of clients served by nonprofit								
Other								

Figure 6 continued on page 17.

Board Profile and Analysis

Because organizational needs drive a board diversity initiative, the planning phase should include a profile and analysis of the current board. It is helpful to use a criteria matrix like the one in figure 6. By completing such a worksheet, board members will be able to see clearly what attributes, skills, and talents are important to the present and future of the organization. This exercise also helps identify the gaps in the board's composition in a nonthreatening, organization-driven way.

To use this tool effectively, customize it to the organization. Decide what criteria should be added or eliminated based on current needs and plans. Either ask each board member or assign a committee to assess the characteristics and skills of current board members, and then note any gaps in skills, ethnicity, geographic area, age, or other characteristics.

With the information gleaned from the board profile, analyze the board in light of organizational decision-making roles (figure 7). Who actually leads the board and makes decisions on behalf of the organization? How well is the board using the skills available among its members? Who participates in developmental opportunities such as conferences and workshops? Who represents the organization in various settings, and why?

The information gathered from the board profile and analysis should help clarify board diversity issues. The board may also want to examine demographic information on users of the organization's programs and services and the geographic service area, so that areas needing immediate attention can be given priority.

Developing a Plan

The results of the organizational assessment and board profile and analysis will begin to define the scope and nature of the organization's issues in the area of board diversity. The board must now develop short- and long-term plans that will position the organization to build a diverse board. Effective plans will cover at least 6 to 18 months.

The diversity initiative plan should

■ set clear and attainable goals and objectives;

■ establish a structure and timetables;

■ encourage teamwork and shared leadership;

■ require an investment of board members' time and energy; and

■ make board members aware of their contribution to success.

Figure 6 (continued)
Board Profile Worksheet

CATEGORIES TO CONSIDER	CURRENT BOARD MEMBERS (199_)				PROSPECTIVE BOARD MEMBERS (199_–_)			
Personal characteristics	1	2	3	4	A	B	C	D
Ages ▲ *Under 35*								
▲ *From 35 to 50*								
▲ *From 51 to 65*								
▲ *Over 65*								
Gender ▲ *Women*								
▲ *Men*								
Physical disability								
Sexual orientation								
Race/ethnic background								
▲ *Asian/Pacific Islander*								
▲ *Black/African American*								
▲ *Hispanic/Latino*								
▲ *Native American*								
▲ *Caucasian*								
▲ *Other*								
Geographical location (depending on your mission)								
▲ *City*								
▲ *Suburbs*								
▲ *State*								
▲ *Regional*								
▲ *National*								
▲ *International*								
Financial position								
▲ *Self-employed*								
▲ *Salaried*								
▲ *Philanthropic reputation*								
▲ *Prospective major donor*								

* This chart was adapted from *Six Keys to Recruiting, Orienting, and Involving Nonprofit Board Members* by Judith Grummon Nelson (Washington, DC: National Center for Nonprofit Boards, 1991, 58 pages).

Figure 7

Organizational Decision-Makers Profile Worksheet

The board profile worksheet (Figure 6) can help create a profile of the entire board. The following chart allows you to look at some specific characteristics of key board leaders. You might also use this chart to create a profile of a single committee, such as the nominating committee or the executive committee.

NAME	COMMITTEE/ROLE	WHITE	BLACK/AFRICAN AMERICAN	HISPANIC/LATINO	NATIVE AMERICAN	ASIAN/PACIFIC ISLANDER	MALE	FEMALE	GAY/LESBIAN	DISABLED

It may be advisable for a small group, such as the task force described in chapter 2 or the nominating committee, to develop the plan with the assistance of key staff. Consider involving people from outside the organization who have skill and expertise in this area.

The plan must be ambitious and challenging and yet incorporate opportunities for success so that progress will be evident. Setting goals and developing short- and long-term objectives will help. Given the strategic and long-term focus of building a diverse board, consider articulating a "vision" for the initiative that expresses some broad needs based on the results of the planning phase. For example, the board may decide that there is a need to develop or enhance the organization's visible commitment to diversity. One short-term objective may be to review, reaffirm, or revise the organizational mission to ensure that it reflects such a commitment.

By building success into the short-term objectives of the plan, the board will help prevent backlash and reinforce the idea that achieving diversity is not an impossible endeavor. The point is to think big but make sure the plan includes manageable steps. Milestones and mechanisms to evaluate progress are also important. Plans are made to be used, so progress should be measured periodically and contingency plans put into place when objectives are not met.

By the end of the planning phase, the board has made a commitment to undertaking a diversity initiative. The success of the initiative depends on board leaders' ability to help other board members translate commitment into action. Board members must expand their awareness, clarify their assumptions, and increase their sensitivity to the complex questions involved in building board diversity. They must learn about the changing demographics and other external factors that often are the catalyst for a diversity initiative. They need to understand why it is essential to address board diversity now and what the implications of change are for the organization.

Board members' awareness can develop in many ways. As a foundation, board leaders who are guiding the initiative should set a positive tone and create an atmosphere in which board members feel comfortable expressing both their support for the initiative and their concerns. When candor is encouraged, board members will then be better able to discuss the issues. Formal activities also will build awareness. Meetings, workshops, and training programs provide opportunities to present information, assess progress, and develop the skills of individual board members. The board and the organization as a whole will profit from thorough organizational and board assessments.

Informational Meetings

The diversity initiative task force may schedule one- to two-hour informational meetings throughout the process or incorporate such meetings into the agenda of particular board meetings.. The participants may be a mix of board, key staff, and advisory group members. Each meeting should have specific objectives and an agenda (Figure 8). At the discretion of the task force, participants may receive written materials before each meeting.

For many organizations, the early informational meetings are the first opportunity to engage the board in a discussion of diversity. The content and structure of these meetings must be such that board members leave with a greater sense of clarity about what diversity means, why the organization needs to address the issue now, and how building an inclusive board will have a positive impact on the organization's ability to fulfill its mission. At strategic intervals throughout the initiative, informational meetings are forums for discussing progress. Board members can review the outcomes of activities and exchange ideas on developing appropriate contingency plans or next steps.

Workshops and Training Programs

Many organizations hold a "Building a Diverse Board" workshop or training program as a way of introducing the topic to the board, developing board members' awareness, and presenting action steps that the board can take, collectively and individually (Figure 9). Action steps enable the board to foster diversity and recruit and retain the best possible talent. As much as possible, they should build on or reflect organizational plans.

When designing an effective training program, consider the following guidelines:

■ Training programs are methods of accomplishing certain objectives. They are not final products or outcomes.

■ Customize training to meet the needs of the organization.

■ Set objectives that are ambitious yet achievable within the allocated time.

■ Hold the training in private locations with few distractions. Participants should have few, if any, interruptions.

■ When possible, deliver a training program in a full day. The module approach, although workable, may not have the full effect, and multiple sessions may not always include the same participants.

■ Provide challenging program content, but welcome participants' involvement. By the end of the program, each participant should feel that he or she can do something to help the board move forward in building diversity.

Figure 8
Informational Meetings Worksheet

Informational meetings will be one to two hours long. They should be held throughout the diversity initiative.

Purpose

Objective(s)

1.

2.

Participants

Date and location

Materials needed

▲   *To be sent to participants before the meeting:*

▲   *To be distributed at the meeting:*

Suggested format

▲   *Overview and introductions*

▲   *Agenda review*

▲   *Objectives review*

▲   *Presentation of topic(s) and reports*

▲   *Implications for the organization's diversity initiative*

▲   *Discussion*

▲   *Agreement on actions and next steps*

▲   *Summary*

Figure 9
Training Programs Worksheet

Title
_____

Purpose
_____

Objective(s)

1. _____

2. _____

3. _____

4. _____

Total length
_____

Content

SEGMENT	LEARNING OBJECTIVE	TIME	DELIVERY METHOD
1.			
2.			
3.			
4.			
5.			
6.			
7.			
8.			

Number of participants
_____

Audiovisual requirements
_____

Room set-up
_____

Other requirements *(e.g., flip chart and easel, markers, tape, 3 x 5 cards, nametags, tent cards)*
_____

Pre-workshop assignments for participants
_____

■ Select varied and interactive presentation methods.

■ Ask participants for written evaluations at the end of the program. These evaluations should, at a minimum, measure the participants' reactions to the program, trainer, and materials. They should also highlight some of the most useful tools.

■ Make follow-up and reinforcement activities part of the training plan. It will be important to plan and budget for additional work.

A training program should cover the following topics:

■ an explanation of diversity

■ the importance of diversity to the organization

■ the benefits to the board

■ the phases in developing a diverse board

■ board analysis activities

■ helping individual board members prepare for diversity

■ taking action

Choosing a Trainer or Facilitator

The trainer or facilitator who designs and conducts a diversity workshop needs considerable abilities and experience in both diversity and board development processes. In addition, he or she should be able to:

■ articulate honestly what the board can expect from the training program given the organizational assessment, the length of time allocated, and the program logistics;

■ demonstrate knowledge and experience in group process learning and facilitation;

■ create an environment in which board members are willing to participate, not overwhelmed by what they have *not* done, and motivated to take the next steps;

■ respond effectively and skillfully to people from various cultures, even without specific or detailed information about the cultures;

■ recognize his or her own cultural values and use them in informative, not judgmental, ways; and

■ communicate clearly using simple language.

Organizational Culture and Board Roles

Organizations that truly want to be effective in building a diverse board should not stop at developing individual board members' awareness and skills. Preparing the organization and creating a supportive organizational climate are critical to success. A thorough assessment of organizational culture and board roles and responsibilities can pave the way.

Every organization has formal documents, including its mission statement, bylaws, and written policies and procedures, that characterize it both internally and externally. Organizational culture—defined as shared internal values, beliefs, and expectations—further characterizes an organization. These values, beliefs, and expectations often are unwritten and informal. Nevertheless, they affect every part of the organization and result in norms and standards that determine the behavior of the individuals and groups within it.

In their book *Corporate Cultures,* Terrence Deal and Allan Kennedy note four dimensions of organizational culture that may help board members understand the impact it has on building a diverse board:

1. values (the basic beliefs of the organization)

2. heroes and heroines (the symbolic figures who model the types of behavior that are desirable in the organization)

3. traditions and rituals (the activities that the board and the organization regularly engage in)

4. cultural network (the informal communication network that provides information and interprets messages sent through the organization)

Another dimension of organizational culture is conflict management, or the ways in which disagreements and conflicts are handled. Conflict management also addresses what happens when hidden or personal agendas surface.

If the board has not done so recently, it should review board functions—the role of the board in the organization and the responsibilities of board members (Figure 10). Board members also should decide if they need to review board systems—the processes and procedures by which the board does its work.

The assessment of organizational culture and board roles and responsibilities can be formal or informal. The questionnaire in Figure 11 will help board members in this exploration.

Figure 10
Basic Responsibilities of Nonprofit Boards

1. Determine the organization's mission and purposes.
2. Select the chief executive.
3. Support the chief executive and review his or her performance.
4. Ensure effective organizational planning.
5. Ensure adequate resources.
6. Manage resources effectively.
7. Determine and monitor the organization's programs and services.
8. Enhance the organization's public image.
9. Serve as a court of appeal.
10. Assess its own performance.

This list was taken from *Ten Basic Responsibilities of Nonprofit Boards* by Richard T. Ingram (Washington, DC: National Center for Nonprofit Boards, 1988, 22 pages).

Self-Assessment for Nonprofit Governing Boards, a publication of the National Center for Nonprofit Boards, provides additional assistance in analyzing board functions and board members' responsibilities.

Conduct the assessment after the diversity initiative is under way rather than in the beginning phases. This timing has distinct advantages. Board members have increased their understanding of and sensitivity to cultural diversity issues. They should be better prepared to discuss the role the organization's environment plays in building a diverse board. If board members spend too much time in organizational assessment at the beginning of the initiative, they may become discouraged or lose interest. They may also be disheartened if too many areas needing improvement surface early. Planning for the board to accomplish some short-term objectives early in the initiative may increase board members' receptivity to an in-depth examination of more complex organizational issues.

Once the board has examined the dimensions of the organization's culture and reviewed board functions and systems, the next step is to determine the barriers to building a diverse board and the opportunities inherent in the process. Barriers are any values, norms, practices, and policies that hinder or prevent those with different, yet equally valid, perspectives from becoming fully participatory board members. Opportunities exist in values, norms, practices, and policies that are welcoming or are flexible enough to allow those with different perspectives to become fully participatory board members.

Of course, not all values, norms, practices, and policies will have to change. For example, one of the board's basic beliefs may be "We are family." This belief may represent an organizational barrier to those who do not look or act like the traditional family member. But it may also present an opportunity for building diversity if the organization embraces anyone joining the board, including those who are culturally different, as though they truly are vital to the organization.

Whatever the organizational culture and board functions, practices, and systems are, it is paramount to board members' success to share this information. The more informed a board member is about what the organization values and what is expected, the more productive he or she can be as a board member. If there is any conflict between the organization's culture and a board member's culture, it will be most beneficial to both the organization and the board member to discuss it openly and try to resolve it before major problems start to occur.

Changing organizational culture is not easy. It takes time. It can be overwhelming because the values, norms, and expectations of an organization are its very heart. Nevertheless, a board that does not take the time to discuss, analyze, and make the appropriate adjustments to its culture may undermine all other efforts to build diversity.

Figure 11

Organizational Audit Questionnaire *(This tool will be useful when combined with a review of board functions and responsibilities.)*

PART 1 ORGANIZATIONAL CULTURE ANALYSIS

Values

1. What are the values that the organization considers most important? Include those that are actually considered important, not just those that are written.

2. Do most board members share these values?

3. What values/messages do the organization's publications convey?

Heroes/Heroines

4. What types of behavior does the organization desire and value?

5. Who on this board models the behavior that the organization desires and values? Past board members can be included.

Traditions and Rituals

6. What are the organization's traditions?

7. What types of activities does the board engage in monthly, quarterly, annually?

8. Which of these activities are considered of critical importance to a board member's success?

9. What other organizational activities are board members expected to attend or depend heavily upon board members' participation?

10. What rituals does the board participate in that represent the ideals of the organization?

11. a. Do board members socialize outside board-related activities?

    b. If so, are board matters discussed at these social occasions?

    c. What type of events are these activities, and who is invited to attend?

Figure 11 continued on page 26.

Figure 11 (continued)

Organizational Audit Questionnaire *(This tool will be useful when combined with a review of board functions and responsibilities.)*

PART 1—ORGANIZATIONAL CULTURE ANALYSIS (CONTINUED)

Conflict Management

12. How does the board handle conflict between members?

13. How are disagreements resolved?

14. How is anger handled?

15. How do hidden or personal agendas become known?

16. What role(s) do hidden and personal agendas play in decision making for the board?

PART 2—BOARD SYSTEMS AND PROCEDURES ANALYSIS

17. How are board members nominated and selected for board membership?

18. What type of orientation takes place for new members?

19. How are new members integrated into the organization?

20. What materials are given to new members?

21. What is the time commitment necessary to be an effective board member?

22. a. Do board members attend meetings and workshops outside of the organization?

    b. If so, who attends these meetings?

23. How are committee and ad hoc group leaders chosen?

24. What is the role of the board chair?

Figure 11 continued on page 27.

Figure 11 (continued)

Organizational Audit Questionnaire

PART 2—BOARD SYSTEMS AND PROCEDURES ANALYSIS (CONTINUED)

25. Does the board have a system for rotating members off the board? Are there staggered terms?

26. a. Do former board members play a role in the organization?

    b. If so, what is (are) their role(s)?

27. Are exit interviews conducted with board members who resign or rotate off the board?

28. Does the board evaluate individual board members' participation?

29. a. Are board members ever terminated by the organization?

    b. If so, under what circumstances?

Notes

The early phases of the diversity initiative may reveal that the board has work to do before taking action to make the board more inclusive. Boards that already make ongoing board cultivation, recruitment, and retention a high priority will have an easier time incorporating the goal of inclusiveness into the existing practices and procedures of their nominating committees than those that do not have a well-developed process. A long-term endeavor such as achieving and sustaining board diversity requires time, attention, and consistent effort.

Recruiting Board Members

Unfortunately, many boards do not think about who should be the volunteer leaders of the organization until a few months or even weeks before the annual meeting at which elections are held. Board recruitment is such a crucial task, yet many boards do not even have active nominating committees, orientation for new members, and other practices that help them identify, select, and retain effective board members (see Figure 12).

When beginning to recruit new members from diverse backgrounds, the board's first task is to lay the groundwork. It takes time to build trust and establish relationships within communities. It also takes time to locate just the right people. Board members should make their presence known and begin to participate in appropriate community-related activities long before they begin to recruit new members. Other organizations and individuals in the community can help by sharing their experiences. Staff, board members, volunteer recruitment groups, community leaders, consultants, and advisory group members can advise the board on the types of outreach efforts that will best position the organization in the community given limited time and resources.

As they work to heighten the organization's profile and increase community involvement, board members may find out things they did not know about the community's perceptions. They may have to be prepared to hear about how invisible the organization has been in the past. Be honest in discussing the issues. If this perception is true, acknowledge it and move on.

An understanding of the meaning and implications of diversity is critical to the recruitment effort. Race, ethnicity, gender, age, and other factors are attributes of a diverse board. Board members also need skills, talents, time, and commitment. The board should not assume that building diversity means sacrificing skills for attributes. Such an assumption is a disservice to the organization and to prospective board members who have both attributes and skills to offer.

Similarly, it is important to understand that representation does not mean tokenism. Building a diverse board does not involve setting quotas. Remember as well that groups are internally diverse and that one member cannot speak for everyone in that group. Recruit, welcome, and involve new board members based on their perspectives and experiences, but involve them in activities based on their individual skills, talents, and interests.

Sound board member recruitment practices work for all new board members. An ongoing emphasis on recruitment will help an organization find the best prospective board members and cultivate their interest in board service. The NCNB publication *The Nominating Committee: Laying a Foundation for Your Organization's Future* is a useful resource in a board diversity initiative.

Retaining Board Members

Retaining diverse board members is the test of how well the organization is living up to its commitment to inclusiveness. Boards that take the time to be successful at retention will find that they have given their organizations a competitive edge in building a diverse board.

The cornerstone of retention is board development, which establishes a welcoming organizational climate and helps new board members become part of the organization in meaningful ways.

The organization will be well on its way to creating an environment in which *all* board members feel welcomed and valued when it pays attention to the various aspects of board development, including

■ conducting a thorough orientation for new members that includes a reaffirmation of the commitment to diversity;

■ giving new members adequate and timely information and materials;

■ engaging board members in meaningful board activities; and

■ soliciting reactions from members on how the systems and procedures are working for them and adjusting the processes and policies that hinder full participation.

An effective orientation program will help new board members become fully acclimated to the organizational culture, functions, and tasks board members must perform. Make sure that the new member clearly understands the responsibilities and expectations of board service before he or she joins the board, and then continue the learning process during orientation and beyond. To ease orientation, many organizations have designed coaching and buddy systems pairing more seasoned board members with new members. Individuals are

Figure 12
Pointers for Recruiting and Retaining a Diverse Board

1. Be prepared to devote time, attention, and consistent effort to board recruitment and retention.
2. Be honest in discussing the issues.
3. Look to build relationships that foster trust and alliances.
4. Look for skills as well as attributes in prospective board members.
5. Engage new board members in meaningful activities based on their skills, talents, and interests.
6. Follow sound board development practices to create a positive working climate for *all* board members.

"Once on the board, it is easy to feel isolated. There is a need for organizations to make the individual feel part of the organization."

matched according to board tasks, areas of responsibility, interests, geographic location, and developmental opportunities.

The board should also consider the ways in which board members interact beyond board meetings. Invite new members to attend social activities that are strategic in positioning the board or the organization within the community. If they decline to participate, do not assume they are being uncooperative. There may be a number of reasons why, and it may be useful to find out what those reasons are.

New board members can become involved in the diversity initiative, too. Engage them in a discussion of the initiative and help them understand the level of organizational commitment. Include them in informational meetings and discussions about the next steps in building a diverse board. Invite them to serve on appropriate committees, task forces, advisory panels, and other ad hoc groups that are developing and monitoring

plans in the diversity initiative. The board chair, *chief executive*, and other leaders of the initiative should seek out new members' opinions regularly.

After taking the time to recruit and orient board members from diverse backgrounds who have the requisite skills and talent, do not let these assets go to waste. New members should begin at once to be involved in the work of the board through committees, task forces, and meetings of the full board. Expect no more or no less from board members based on differences in attributes. Both experienced and new board members share in the responsibility to ensure successful relationships.

Board self-assessment is another tool that can help all board members understand their roles. A regular review of how well the board has met its responsibilities will give board members valuable information about what is expected of them, and it can help them determine their roles in meeting some of the challenges the board faces.

At the very least, the board chair or chief executive should have follow-up conversations with new board members before the end of the first year of service. Their conversations give new members an opportunity to express their feelings about being on the board. Like the self-assessment process, this effort also brings to light what the board is doing well and reveals the obstacles to full board participation. The discussion can be formal or informal.

A written checklist for the new member is a good starting point. The National Center for Nonprofit Boards publication *Six Keys to Recruiting, Orienting, and Involving Nonprofit Board Members* includes a sample checklist.

and the chief executive, can hold a brainstorming session that includes those affected by the patterns or trends. Other board members should attend only if they have a particular reason for being there.

> *"A specific commitment of time and money to addressing issues of diversity among boards is needed in order to educate current board members and for leadership development."*

If self-assessment or follow-up reveals a pattern or trend that there is a lack of participation from various groups of new *or* experienced board members, the board chair and chief executive should meet with the individual members involved. When corrective action needs to be explored, a small group of the board, including the board chair

Once the board decides on and commits to action steps, it should make changes as swiftly as possible. The board may be able to retain valuable board members who are skeptical or discouraged if a sincere, good-faith effort is apparent.

The implications of board diversity for a nonprofit organization are profound. When the stakes are so high, it makes sense to incorporate evaluation into the diversity initiative from the start. The evaluation results can help the board shape the process and ultimately be used to design future phases.

Evaluation

Several evaluation mechanisms have been noted so far in this publication, including informational meetings; training program evaluation; a review of the action steps developed by training program participants; board self-assessment; and follow-up and informal feedback from new board members.

Build evaluation into the overall plan for a diversity initiative. The plan should include milestones for measuring progress of the various phases and activities. These milestones can be both specific, time-framed, measurable objectives that are examined once a year, or more frequently.

The board may decide to engage in a formal evaluation led by an outside evaluator. The evaluator should meet the criteria for a board diversity consultant described in chapter 2 and be skilled and experienced in evaluation methods and processes. Or the board may design its own evaluation guided by board leaders, the chief executive, and senior staff.

Whatever the method, the results must include honest, clear, and useful information highlighting accomplishments and work remaining to be done. The board must be committed to using the evaluation results to make improvements and build on their successes. The board may also want to let the organization's constituency and funding sources know about the accomplishments reported in the evaluation.

Beyond the Initial Cycle

After the first round of recruitment and orientation is complete, board members are ready to decide what they would like to happen next. The existing vision, mission, and evaluation results can be the starting points for deciding what the board wants to accomplish during subsequent phases of the diversity initiative. Time, resources, available skills and talents, and coordination with other organizational plans will also be factors. The board may want to mark the continuation of the initiative by publicly reaffirming its commitment to building a diverse board. This statement reinforces the fact that achieving diversity is a cyclical, ongoing, long-term process, not a program.

Continue holding informational meetings as the initiative progresses. These meetings are critical to keeping everyone engaged and informed as well as to redesigning the initiative or redirecting activities. The involvement of board members, key staff, and advisory group members will enhance the level of discussion.

Plan follow-up and reinforcement activities for the training received during the initial phases so that board members can continue to build their skills and cultural competencies. Determine what additional training board members need based on the problems or challenges they faced in taking action to build diversity.

At this stage, the board will be a more diverse team, and board members' varied perspectives should help to increase sensitivity and awareness within the board. Training can be expanded to feature team building and leadership development activities, which will help the board move from being a well-managed group to a diverse team of organizational leaders.

Some changes to the organizational culture, systems, and board functions will naturally occur in the first cycle of building a diverse board. Nevertheless, as the initiative progresses the board should work actively to institutionalize these changes and redefine the dimensions of the organization's culture, as appropriate. Institutionalizing change involves

■ ensuring that organizational values are clear and lived by rather than just written;
■ adjusting traditions and rituals so that they are inclusive;
■ identifying new heroes and heroines as they emerge; and
■ establishing a communication network that is open and maintains integrity.

The board can provide a model for staff diversity and inclusive behavior. Ensuring that board practices are ethical, consistent, and fair in the treatment of members and that board functions and members' responsibilities are based on skills, talents, and interests contribute to creating an organization that values diversity.

Now that the board has spent much of its time in self-examination, reviewing and redesigning systems, and, in general, preparing itself to become more diverse, the plans for the next cycle may expand to include an increase in the number and types of community outreach efforts. Develop activities that will strengthen the commitment to building diversity and continue to strategically position the organization for change.

"One of the most effective strategies for getting culturally diverse groups into our performing arts center and, ultimately, for identifying those who could have a long-term relationship with the center was to collaborate with two other organizations from the community. We put together a plan that provided visibility, exposure, and resources to all three organizations."

Other organizations that have similar missions, programs, and services but different audiences or constituencies can be good partners. Seek out relationships with diverse organizations. Consider collaborative efforts that will promote a better response to the entire community's needs while strengthening both organizations. Cosponsoring or becoming involved in community events involving diverse racial and ethnic groups also offers potential. Such events can open new horizons for the board, or they provide the opportunity to reinforce activities that the organization already undertakes. If the board has used an advisory group during the diversity initiative, it may want to develop additional groups to advise on issues such as fund raising and strategic planning.

In general, board members and advisory group members should be active community ambassadors and advocates of the diversity initiative. Board members can speak to other organizations about achieving success. Board leaders and the chief executive should help board members be well informed so that their outreach in the community is as effective as possible.

Building a diverse board is as strategic an issue as any other confronting today's nonprofit organization. It is also complex and evolving, and it can test the board's capacity for dialogue, candor, and sensitivity to differing viewpoints. Each organization must decide what it must do to develop a diverse board and how its actions in this area affect those in other areas. Remember that success is a journey, not a destination, and that building board diversity is a cyclical process. Whenever and however the board decides to begin the journey, the first step must be taken. The organization's future depends on it. ■

American Association of Museums

Excellence and Equity: Education and the Public Dimension of Museums. Washington, DC: AAM, 1991.

A report emphasizing a broader mission for museums: to undertake a museum-wide effort by staff, trustees, and volunteers to serve the public through education and activities that reflect their diverse communities. It outlines ten principles related to this endeavor and recommends strategies to achieve excellence and equity.

American Symphony Orchestra League (ASOL)

A Survey and Study by the American Symphony Orchestra League. Washington, DC: ASOL, 1991.

Results of a study of 329 orchestra boards of directors, including their composition and committee structure. It presents a profile of board members by age, gender, and race.

Carson, Emmett D.

Black Volunteers as Givers and Fundraisers. New York: The Center for the Study of Philanthropy, 1990.

Discusses how the extent to which black volunteers are actively engaged in giving and fundraising relates to the amount of effort a nonprofit organization expends in recruiting black and other minority volunteers. The paper also raises questions about the impact of race on the size of charitable contributions and examines traditions and forms of philanthropy in the black community.

Council on Foundations

Donors of Color. Washington, DC: Council on Foundations, 1993.

A study to examine philanthropic trends among donors of color (African Americans, Asians, and Hispanics) and how community foundations can develop programs to serve and recruit donors of color.

Council on Foundations

The Inclusive Community: A Handbook for Managing Diversity in Community Foundations. Washington, DC: Council on Foundations, 1992.

A guide to the importance of including and reaching out to all facets of the public in fulfilling a community foundation's mission. Sections relating to mission, governance, personnel policies, grantmaking, resource development, and communications cite examples to encourage inclusive practices.

Deal, Terrence and Kennedy, Allan

Corporate Cultures. Reading, MA: Addison–Wesley, 1982.

Examines the role of organizational culture in organizational life. Notes the dimensions of organizational culture and explores the ways in which these dimensions characterize the organization to those inside and outside it.

Fernandez, Aileen C.

National Women of Color Organizations. New York: The Ford Foundation, 1991.

A study of nonprofit organizations that focus on women of color. Twenty-three organizations are identified. Most stress leadership development, employment opportunities, improved education, strengthening of the family, and economic development.

Gallegos, Herman and O'Neill, Michael, eds.

Hispanics and the Nonprofit Sector. New York: The Foundation Center, 1991.

A compilation of papers assessing the history, role, and impact of Hispanic and Latino nonprofit organizations. Focuses on the contributions of organizations in the legal, political, social service, cultural, and educational fields, as well as the role of women and religion in nonprofit organizations.

Hirzy, Ellen Cochran

The Nominating Committee: Laying a Foundation for Your Organization's Future. Washington, DC: National Center for Nonprofit Boards, 1994.

This booklet illuminates the nominating committee's responsibilities, including its role in cultivating and developing the board. Also discussed are guidelines for its size and composition, committee planning, and evaluating its performance.

Houle, Cyril O.

Governing Boards: Their Nature and Nurture. San Francisco: Jossey-Bass Publishers, Inc., 1989. (Also available from the National Center for Nonprofit Boards.)

Provides advice on a variety of issues facing nonprofit boards, including board structure and education, board/staff roles, and challenges for the nonprofit sector.

Ingram, Richard T.

Ten Basic Responsibilities of Nonprofit Boards. Washington, DC: National Center for Nonprofit Boards, 1988.

A booklet that describes the fundamental responsibilities of nonprofit boards, focusing primarily on the whole board as a single entity.

Jamestown Area Labor Management Committee (JALMC)

"Managing Diversity." Jamestown, NY: JALMC.

Monthly source of information, ideas, and tips for people managing a diverse workforce.

Jamieson, David and O'Mara, Julie

Managing Workforce 2000: Gaining the Diversity Advantage. San Francisco: Jossey-Bass, 1991.

This book is designed to help executives and managers understand the changing workforce so that they can manage more effectively.

Leadership Education for Asian Pacifics (LEAP).

The State of Asian Pacific America: A Public Policy Report: Policy Issues to the Year 2020.
Los Angeles: LEAP, 1992.

A study that collects the different perspectives of Asian Pacific American experts from universities and community organizations throughout the country.

Odendahl, Teresa and O'Neill, Michael, eds.

Women and Power in the Nonprofit Sector. San Francisco: Jossey-Bass Publishers, Inc., 1994.

A collection of essays on women in the voluntary sector from a variety of viewpoints: women as nonprofit employees and volunteers; the effects of the women's movement on women's status in nonprofits; and the impact of gender, social class, and race on women in the nonprofit sector.

Oomkes, Frank R. and Thomas, Richard H.

"Cross Cultural Communication Skills Training Activities." Fredonia, NY:
Connaught/HR Press, 1992.

Contains workshop designs for communicating across cultures.

Robinson, Maureen K.

Developing the Nonprofit Board: Strategies for Orienting, Educating and Motivating Board Members.
Washington, DC: National Center for Nonprofit Boards, 1994.

A book outlining a variety of activities to develop a nonprofit board. It offers strategies to engage the board in orienting new members, conducting training sessions, and evaluating its performance.

Rogers, Pier and Palmer, John

Nonprofit Management and Leadership: The Status of People of Color. San Francisco: Nonprofit Academic Centers Council, 1993.

A study of staff diversity in three workforces: government, corporate, and nonprofit. Researchers found that nonprofit organizations have the least diverse staffs, where most members of minority groups hold lower-ranking jobs as compared to government and corporate workplaces, where higher percentages of minorities hold higher-level jobs.

Shue, Sylvia, Smith, Bradford and Villareal, Joseph

Asian and Hispanic Philanthropy. San Francisco: University of San Francisco, 1992.

A study of the customs surrounding the donation of gifts, money, and services by several Asian and Hispanic communities in the San Francisco Bay area. Focuses on how the cultural dimensions of gift-giving, financial assistance, sharing, and the distribution of income and wealth differ in meaning from culture to culture.

Simons, Dr. George F.

The Questions of Diversity. Amherst, MA: ODT Incorporated, 1992.

A collection of assessment tools for organizations and individuals.

Taylor, Charles A.

The Guide to Multicultural Resources 1993/1994. Fort Atchinson, WI: Highsmith Press, 1994.

A comprehensive guide of information, including statistics and organizational listings, that tracks activity in multicultural communities. Focuses on African-American/Black, Hispanic/Latino, Asian/Pacific and Native American resources.

Thomas, Jr., R. Roosevelt

Beyond Race and Gender. New York: American Management Association, 1992.

This book led the way in focusing organizations on the "roots" of corporate culture as they relate to diversity.

United Way of Greater Toronto

Action, Access, Diversity! Toronto: United Way of Greater Toronto, 1991.

A guide to multicultural/anti-racist organizational change for social service agencies. This model strives to enhance an organization's ability to engage and respond to its community's diversity.

United Way of New York City

Linkages: Building Effective Multi-Cultural Boards. New York: United Way of New York City.

A guide designed to assist in increasing the number of minority representatives on the governing boards of social service agencies. The materials focus on recruitment, orientation, and continuing education for minority board members once they join a board.

Women & Philanthropy

Far from Done: The Challenge of Diversifying Philanthropic Leadership. New York: Women and Foundations/Corporate Philanthropy, 1990.

One in a series of titles, this book examines foundation boards (private, community, and corporate) by race and gender. This data is accompanied by a series of articles focusing on foundation board diversity, women on foundation boards, and two studies of foundation governing boards.

Work, Dr. W. John

Toward Affirmative Action and Racial/Ethnic Pluralism. Arlington, VA: The Belvedere Press, 1989.

Trainer's workshop on affirmative action, institutional racism and pluralism.

American National Red Cross

Guidelines for Outreach to Minority Populations.

A guide for Red Cross chapters in encouraging members of the diverse population to participate as providers or recipients of Red Cross services. Sections focus on developing outreach programs, forming advisory committees, and initiating minority recruitment programs.

United Way of America

Building Volunteer Diversity: Project Blueprint.

A program of curricula developed by the United Way that has been implemented in numerous cities across the U.S. Project Blueprint strives to increase the participation of Hispanic, Asian, Black, and Native American communities in United Way activities by training United Way staff, volunteers, and community-based organizations to heighten awareness of culturally-sensitive issues.

A Summary of NCNB's
Research on Board Diversity

An important aspect of the Board Diversity Project was the opportunity to take a snapshot of the status of diversity issues inside the nonprofit sector and at the board level. To help bring the image into focus, NCNB solicited information from board members about their experiences, conducted a survey, and read and reviewed the research and literature produced on diversity in the nonprofit sector.

Giachello and Associates, a Chicago-based social research and staff development firm, designed and conducted the research activities. The work of the firm's principals, Aida L. Giachello, Mara T. Patermaster and Donna Ruscavage, was invaluable to the project. Each of the research initiatives gave NCNB a sense of the issues that affect board diversity and inclusiveness, and helped us to shape the content of this booklet and the focus of related services.

Background

In January 1992, NCNB received a grant from the Ford Foundation to develop training materials and publications to assist nonprofit organizations to develop more diverse governing boards. The initiative, which became known as the Board Diversity Project, included funding for an assessment of the current status of nonprofit organizations in achieving board diversity.

NCNB engaged Giachello and Associates, Inc, a minority- and women-owned firm, to conduct a series of research activities. The purposes of the research component of the Board Diversity Project were:

■ To assess current levels of knowledge, attitudes and behaviors of nonprofit organizations regarding diversity issues;

■ To document selected indicators of board recruitment and major areas of difficulty in establishing culturally diverse boards; and,

■ To identify areas where nonprofits need technical assistance and training in building board diversity.

Table IA:
Characteristics of Individuals Responding to the Survey

	PERCENT	NUMBER OF CASES
Relationship to organization		
Board member	1.1%	7
Board officer	1.8	11
Chief executive	88.5	548
Other staff	8.6	51
Sex		
Female	65	402
Male	35	216
Race/ethnicity		
White/Caucasian	93.2	575
Black/African American	2.9	18
Hispanic/Latino	2.4	15
Native American	.3	2
Other	.8	5

Table IB:
Characteristics of Organizations Responding to the Survey

	PERCENT	NUMBER OF CASES
Year founded		
Before 1900	2.7%	17
1900-1940	11.3	69
1941-1960	12.1	75
1961-1970	16.8	104
1971-1980	28.6	171
1981-1985	12.9	80
1986-1992	15.6	96
Operating budget for 1993		
Less than $250,000	22.4%	137
$250,000 to $499,000	21.2	130
$500,000 to $1 million	23.5	144
$1 million to $5 million	26.6	163
More than $5 million	3.8	23
More than $10 million	2.5	15
Area of work		
Aging	3.6%	22
Health	14.7	90
Mental health	7.4	46
Housing	6.1	37
International affairs	.5	3
Employment	1.6	10
Education	10	62
Youth service and development	11	68
Arts and culture	5.7	35
Communications	.5	3
Public policy	.6	4
Religion	1.3	8
Social action	5.3	33
Conservation	1.6	10
Other	30.1	183

Table IB continued on page 43.

The results included in this appendix are based on data gathered from a national survey of nonprofit organizations, a set of focus groups, and a series of individual interviews with selected representatives of nonprofit organizations.

The national survey

The first nationwide study exploring issues of cultural diversity and their relationship to boards of directors of nonprofit organizations was conducted in July 1993. NCNB mailed questionnaires to 4,208 nonprofit organizations across the United States that were part of NCNB's membership database or publications mailing list.

The researchers used a set of criteria and procedures to ensure a good response rate and to achieve balanced geographic representation of nonprofit organizations. Organizations receiving the survey were selected if:

■ they were a buyer of NCNB publications;

■ the address information included the title of director or chief executive; and

■ the address information included the name of the organization.

Chief executives of organizations in Florida, North Carolina, Virginia, Maryland, New Jersey, Pennsylvania, New York and Massachusetts were included only if their last names began with letters A through M. This criterion was set up to even out the geographical distribution of survey recipients. All organizations meeting the first three criteria in other states were included.

Between July and September, a total of 619 organizations responded to the mail survey. This represented a 14.7% response rate. No follow-up calls or written notices were sent to those who did not reply.

The survey requested information about:

■ the background of respondents and their organizations, including characteristics of staff, clients and board members;

■ how the organization defined diversity;

■ attitudes and behaviors in achieving board diversity;

■ board recruitment practices;

■ respondents' levels of satisfaction with organizational progress in addressing diversity; and

■ organizational need for training and technical assistance.

Survey findings

Characteristics of respondents and their organizations (Tables IA and IB)

■ The majority of respondents were female (65%), chief executives of organizations (88.5%), and White/Caucasian (93.2%).

■ Sixty-seven percent of the organizations had annual operating budgets of less than $1 million.

■ Fifty percent were founded after 1970.

■ The majority of the organizations (about 58%) depend on the private sector as their main source of funding.

■ Responding organizations identified mission areas related to health (14.7%), youth service (11%), education (10%), mental health (7.4%), housing (6.1%), arts and culture (5.7%), and social action/advocacy (5.3%).

■ Most organizations (46.5%) reported their geographic service area to be local, rather than regional or national.

■ The average board size is 21 members. (See Table II for characteristics related to ethnic and cultural diversity.)

Table IB: (continued)

Characteristics of Organizations Responding to the Survey

	PERCENT	NUMBER OF CASES
Primary geographic service area		
National	9.4%	58
Regional	29.9	184
Statewide	14.2	88
Local	46.5	288
Primary ethnic group of *geographic service area*		
White/Caucasian	62.7%	382
Black/African American	6.1	37
Hispanic/Latino	2.6	16
Native American	.5	3
Asian American/Pacific Islander	.6	4
Mix of ethnic/racial groups	27.8	172
Sources of funding *(average for all respondents)*		
Federal government	12.7%	
State government	14	
Local government	14	
Private sector	58.5	
Average number of employees: 38		
Race/ethnicity of *employees* *(average for all respondents)*		
White/Caucasian	77%	
Black/African American	13	
Hispanic/Latino	6	
Native American	1	
Asian American/Pacific Islander	2	
Other	1	

Table II:
Selected Characteristics of the Board of Directors

	AVERAGE NUMBER	NUMBER OF CASES
Board members	21	615
Board members who are:		
White/Caucasian	16.7	603
Black/African American	2.1	604
Hispanic/Latino	.7	595
Native American	.1	595
Asian American/Pacific Islander	.3	599
Women	8.5	606
Elderly (65 and over)	1.8	576
Disabled	.5	581
Individuals of different sexual orientation	.6	412
Youth (under 21)	1	602
Consumers of the organization's services	7	499

Nonprofit organizations and diversity (Tables IIIA, IIIB, IIIC)

■ Respondents provided fairly uniform definitions of the concept of "diversity." The definition given most often referred to the inclusion or representation of racial/ethnic groups and groups that represent different gender or age groups. Few mentioned the inclusion of persons with disabilities or of different sexual orientation or religious beliefs.

■ More than a third of the respondents (36.3%) stated that their board has adopted a policy on cultural diversity.

■ When asked to identify the biggest challenges to the recruitment of individuals from diverse backgrounds as clients, members, or staff (respondents could select multiple answers), 90% of respondents indicated that diversity is not needed because the population served is not diverse; 89% indicated that the organization's mission and goals do not require diversity; 79% indicated a lack of awareness of the importance of diversity among staff and board members.

Attitudes about diversity (Table IV)

■ The majority (71.8%) of respondents felt strongly or very strongly that it was important to have a culturally diverse board.

■ Close to half (47.7%) of respondents believed that most boards are focused on diversity simply to fill quotas or slots.

■ Nearly 90% did not agree or agreed only somewhat that the main reason to build board diversity is to meet funding requirements.

■ Eighty-one percent of respondents believed it was more important to have a mixture of members with different skills and expertise than a culturally diverse board.

■ Between 70 and 75 percent of respondents believed that engaging people of different races or ethnicities in meaningful board activities was not a problem.

Recruitment (Table V)

■ Sixty-nine percent of the organizations reported having some sort of formal procedure for recruitment of board members. The establishment of a nominating committee was the most common procedure used to achieve board diversity (55%).

■ The most frequent eligibility criteria cited were active participation in the organization and attendance at meetings.

■ Forty percent (39.9%) of the organizations reported that annual or frequent financial contributions were required of board members.

■ For those organizations requiring board members' contributions, 84% reported that this requirement did not impede efforts to achieve diversity within the board.

■ More than 50% of the respondents stated that their boards of directors reflected the general makeup of the community they served.

■ The specific activities mentioned to recruit board members from diverse populations included the use of local media, announcements such as those in organizational bulletins, and reaching out to organizations that represent culturally diverse groups.

Satisfaction with board diversity issues (Table VI)

■ Respondents gave mixed reactions regarding satisfaction with achieving diversity in various areas, including client, staff and board. There was substantial dissatisfaction with the organization's achievement of board diversity (58.8%), but less (43.6%) with the board's *commitment* to achieving diversity. Only in the area of the chief executive's involvement in the recruitment of board members was substantial satisfaction expressed (42.9%).

Table IIIA:

Nonprofit Organizations and Diversity

	PERCENT	NUMBER OF CASES
How do you define diversity?		
Representation of racial, ethnic, age groups, gender. . .	17.4%	108
and		
▲ individuals from different education and income levels	7.6	47
▲ individuals with disabilities	2.6	16
▲ individuals of different sexual orientations	5.3	33
▲ individuals from different cultural values and backgrounds	12.3	76
▲ individuals from different geographic areas	2.4	15
▲ individuals from different religious backgrounds	4.2	26
Refers to variety, persons who are different	8.7	54
Is reflective of the community	7.9	49
Other	3.7	23
No answer/no response	27.8	172
Has your board adopted a policy on cultural diversity?		
Yes	36.3%	225
No	60.6	375
No answer	3.1	19
What are the biggest challenges to the recruitment of individuals from diverse backgrounds *as clients, members, or staff*? *(Respondents could select more than one.)*		
Belief that diversity is not needed because the population served is not diverse	90%	560
Belief that the organization's mission and goals do not require diversity	89	550
Lack of awareness of the importance of diversity	79	490
Lack of directives from the board	74	459
Other	64	396
Lack of knowledge on ways to recruit members of diverse groups	50	308

Table IIIB:

Relationship of Staff Diversity to the Diversity of the Community (Geographic Service Area)

	PRIMARY ETHNIC GROUP IN COMMUNITY SERVED[1]					
	White	**Mix**	**Black**	**Latino**	**Native American**	**Asian**
	62%	27.7%	6.2%	2.6%	.6%	.6%
PERCENT OF STAFF WHO ARE:[2]						
White/Caucasian	83.6%	71%	50.6%	47.1%	63%	31.3%
Black/African American	9	17	40.1	9.4	-0-	5.3
Hispanic/Latino	3.4	7.5	3.6	38.4	-0-	12.0
Native American	.49	.52	.11	.06	37	2.8
Asian American/Pacific Islander	.79	1.9	1.9	3.4	-0-	48.7
Other	.46	.89	1.2	-0-	-0-	.89

[1] Based on responses to the question: In the geographic area that you serve, which is the primary ethnic group? See Table IB.

[2] Percentages reflect the reported percentage of staff representing various ethnic groups where that group was identified as the primary group in the community.

Table IIIB correlates staff diversity to the majority population identified by respondents. The chart shows the extent to which the percent of minority staff representation rises as a particular ethnic group is identified as the primary population in a geographic service area. For instance, the percent of African American staff is highest where the primary population was identified as African American.

Table IIIC:

Relationship Between Board Diversity and Diversity of Community (Geographic Service Area)

	PRIMARY ETHNIC GROUP IN COMMUNITY SERVED[1]					
	White	**Mix**	**Black**	**Latino**	**Native American**	**Asian**
	62%	27.7%	6.2%	2.6%	.6%	.6%
AVERAGE NUMBER OF BOARD MEMBERS WHO ARE:[2]						
White/Caucasian	16.8	17.5	14.8	15.8	6	6
Black/African American	1.6	2.46	6.5	2.1	-0-	.5
Hispanic/Latino	.49	.83	.68	3.7	-0-	1.75
Native American	.07	.07	.03	-0-	7.0	.25
Asian American/ Pacific Islander	.17	.35	.32	.27	-0-	5.3

[1] Based on responses to the question: In the geographic area that you serve, which is the primary ethnic group? See Table IB.

[2] Based on the responses to the questions asking for board size (mean number of board members: 21), and for composition of the board (expressed as the mean number of individuals). See Table II.

Table IIIC correlates board diversity to the majority population identified by respondents. A pattern emerges similar to that of the Table IIIB. The highest average number of board members from a particular ethnic group corresponds to the primary ethnic group identified by respondents for their geographic service area. Where the primary population was identified as mixed, the distribution of board members closely resembles the distribution of board members in geographic areas identified as primarily white.

Focus groups

Giachello and Associates conducted two focus groups with representatives of local and national organizations in May 1993. Participants included chief executives and board members of small and large nonprofit organizations, representing both mainstream and ethnic interest institutions in the Washington, D.C., area. Two focus group sessions were conducted to explore critical issues in the area of board diversity. These sessions were both conducted during the same day and each lasted approximately one and a half hours. The focus groups were also used to pre-test the board diversity questionnaire that was later mailed to nonprofit organizations across the country.

The two focus groups targeted different audiences. The first consisted of non-minority board members and staff of mainstream nonprofit organizations in the Washington, D.C., area. Participants were asked to discuss their experiences identifying and recruiting minority board members, and their thoughts and ideas on how to improve retention of diverse board members. Among the chief issues of concern voiced in this focus group were:

■ the need for assistance in identifying pools of prospective candidates for board membership and on ways to gain access to diverse communities;

■ the need to sensitize boards towards diversity other than race and ethnicity, such as age, gender and sexual orientation; and

■ the need to balance fund-raising expectations or contribution requirements with the recruitment of minority candidates to the board.

Table IV:

Respondents' Attitudes Regarding Board Diversity and Related Issues

STATEMENTS	RESPONDENTS' LEVEL OF AGREEMENT (AS A PERCENT OF TOTAL RESPONSES)		
	Strongly or very strongly	Agree	Somewhat or not at all
It is important to have a culturally diverse board of directors.	71.8%	17.7%	10.5%
The most important thing for a board to focus on in diversity is recruitment.	29.1	31.5	39.4
Most boards are focused on diversity simply to fill quotas or slots.	20.6	27.1	52.4
The main reason to achieve board diversity is to meet funding requirements.	5.7	4.7	89.7
It is more important to have ethnic/racial diversity on a board than to have a mix of different skills and expertise.	10.8	8.2	81
It is difficult to retain members from diverse populations once they have been successfully recruited.	13.3	17.1	69.7
It is hard for boards to engage members from racial and ethnic populations in their activities in a meaningful way.	11.6	12.9	75.35

Table V:

Board Membership Recruitment

	PERCENT	NUMBER OF CASES
How does the organization recruit board members?		
Formal procedures (i.e. nominating committee)	54.9%	340
Informal procedures	23.7	147
Formal procedures with broad membership participation	15.5	96
Other	5.7	35
What are eligibility criteria for board membership?		
Active participation, attendance at meetings	20.4%	126
Formal criteria established by board	10.5	65
Resident of geographic area	9.2	57
No criteria established	8.4	52
Financial contributions, fund-raising capabilities	8.2	51
Willingness to serve	7.9	49
Proven leadership, high visibility	6	37
Membership in the organization	5.8	36
Skills needed by the board	4.2	26
Willingness to serve on committees	3.4	21
Client or consumer of the organization's programs	3.1	19
Age (i.e. 21 or older)	1.6	10
Other	1.8	11
No answer	9.5	59
Are frequent financial contributions required?		
Yes	39.9%	247
No	59.8	370
If the answer is yes, do financial contribution requirements impede efforts to achieve diversity?		
Yes	13%	31
No	84	208
No answer/does not apply	3	8
Does the board reflect the general makeup of the community it serves?		
Yes	56.4%	349
No	41.5	257
No answer	2.1	13

Table V continued on page 49.

In the second focus group, which consisted of individuals regularly recruited to serve on boards as representatives of diverse populations, the following issues and concerns emerged during the discussion:

■ the prevalence of tokenism and how this still presents barriers toward retention of board members;

■ the tendency to give more attention to achieving racial and ethnic representation on boards than to the skills individuals can contribute;

■ the need for organizations to understand the meaning of diversity within the context of their purpose and mission, and to have clarity regarding their motives for diversifying; and

■ the need for organizations to invest time and money in achieving diversity as part of an overall organizational strategy.

Both focus groups suggested strategies that organizations could follow to achieve diversity. Chief among them were:

■ Achievement of board diversity should be a goal in the strategic plan for organizations.

■ The composition of the board nominating committee should be diverse and include a mix of board and nonboard members. The criteria for nomination should include items related to skills and expertise as well as to diversity.

■ Organizations should establish board task forces to focus on diversity when designing recruitment strategies.

■ Organizations should establish strong relationships within the community, including neighborhood associations and churches, that would lead to better recruitment of board members.

Individual interviews

Five individuals, each serving on the boards of Washington, D.C.-based organizations, were interviewed by telephone. These individual interviews shared the same purpose as the focus groups, but also sought to elicit a more in-depth assessment of the personal experiences of the interviewees as representatives of diverse populations serving on boards. The individuals, selected by NCNB and the team of researchers, served on a local foundation, a local chapter of a national organization, and in local community-based organizations. Interviews lasted between 30 minutes and one hour.

The interviews were conducted to solicit opinions regarding the major challenges the interviewees perceived to achieving diversity at the board level, as well as to offer suggestions for improving board efforts to achieve diversity. Four of the participants, who represent diverse populations, were also asked to share their experiences as the member of the board who helped achieve diversity.

Only one participant reported that his or her organization had a written policy (in the bylaws) requiring diversity on the board. Four of the five interviewed reported that both the board and staff (typically the chief executive) participated in the recruitment of board members.

Those interviewed reported that the emphasis in achieving diversity was on trying to get the board and staff to be more reflective of the already diverse client population. Among the activities or

Table V: (continued)
Board Membership Recruitment

	PERCENT	NUMBER OF CASES
Does the organization prepare a profile of its board members?		
Yes	62.5%	372
No	37.5	232
What strategies are used to achieve board diversity?		
None	15.8%	98
Tried to recruit minority community members	11.5	71
Established a nominating committee	11.1	69
Obtained input from board and staff	9.2	57
Active recruitment	8.2	51
Identification of organization's needs based on mission	7.4	46
Engage in networking with minority groups	6	37
Advertising/announcements, newspaper, mailing	3.6	22
Informal procedures (i.e. word of mouth)	3.4	21
Use United Way's board leadership resource program	2.4	15
Other	2.4	15
No answer	18.9	117
What activities are used to recruit board members from diverse populations?		
Advertising using local media	28.7%	469
Announcements (i.e. organization's newsletter)	24.1	394
Assistance from organizations representing diverse populations	14.7	241
Requesting assistance from agency staff	13.1	214
Other	19.4	317
What are obstacles to recruiting board members from diverse populations?		
Chief executive has not advised the board to do so, has not emphasized the issue	20.2%	511
Unnecessary because the population being served is not diverse	19.5	494
Not needed because of organization's mission, goals	19.7	497
Lack of awareness of the importance of diversity	15.8	400
Don't know how to identify potential members	10.2	257
Other	14.6	370

Table VI:

Respondents' Levels of Satisfaction with Diversity Issues

HOW SATISFIED ARE YOU . . .	RESPONDENTS' LEVEL OF SATISFACTION (AS A PERCENT OF TOTAL RESPONSES)		
	Not at all or somewhat satisfied	Satisfied	Extremely satisfied, very satisfied
that your organization is achieving diversity among the clients, constituencies that it serves.	38.7%	32.1%	38.3%
that your organization is achieving diversity among its staff.	42.9	25.6	31.4
that your organization is achieving diversity among its board of directors.	58.8	21.9	19.4
with the board's commitment to achieving diversity among its members.	43.6	26	30.4
with plans and activities for recruiting board members from diverse populations.	47.2	28.1	24.7
with the chief executive's level of involvement in the recruitment of board members.	25.9	31.2	42.9
with the orientation your organization gives to new board members, particularly from diverse populations.	40.9	26.5	32.6
with your organization's plans and activities for retention of board members from diverse populations.	39.6	33.1	27.3

strategies suggested to accomplish this were: having people of color chair nominating committees and ensuring the board is committed to the effort; having clearly defined roles and expectations; and not recruiting members only to fill a quota, and which can create a two-tier system on the board, but seeking out individuals on the basis of the skills they bring.

Participants expressed concerns about the processes for retaining and actively involving board members from diverse populations, including: the importance of having a buddy program for new recruits; the need for sensitivity by the "majority" board members in recognizing and understanding the minority position; and striving to ensure that the best individuals for the organization's needs are recruited.

The four individuals representing diverse populations reported mixed experiences as board members. Positive experiences were associated with a number of factors: the level of experience of the chief executive and his or her relationship to the board; and the use of a "personal" approach to board orientation involving a series of informal meetings with the chief executive. Participants expressing a mixed experience cited pressure because of requirements to contribute financially, and not feeling treated as equals (i.e. a sense that the organization had pre-conceived notions regarding Hispanics as lacking education).

Conclusion

The information generated by the research activities was consistently informative for the Board Diversity Project. It helped to clarify a number of issues that influence successful efforts to build a diverse and inclusive board and confirmed the need for strong leadership at the staff and board levels as the process of identifying and recruiting new members proceeds. The research also highlighted the need to view diversity strategically, incorporating it into planning documents, and diversity as an opportunity to build the skill and experience level of the board along with changes in its composition. More than anything, it highlighted the distance those in the nonprofit community feel they need to travel to develop diversity at the board level.

For NCNB and for other individuals and groups, the results reported in the appendix provide a starting point for new research into this important topic. ■

For an up-to-date list of all NCNB publications and information about current prices, membership, and other services, please write or call NCNB at **202-452-6262** (fax 202-452-6299).

▲ *Welcome to the Board: An Orientation Kit for Trustees*

▲ *The Board Member's Guide to Fund Raising* by Fisher Howe

▲ *The Legal Obligations of Nonprofit Boards* by Jacqueline C. Leifer and Michael B. Glomb

▲ *The Financial Responsibilities of Nonprofit Boards* by Andrew S. Lang

▲ *Nonprofit Board Committees* by Ellen Cochran Hirzy

▲ *The Audit Committee* by Sandra Johnson

▲ *The Executive Committee* by Robert Andringa

▲ *The Nominating Committee* by Ellen Cochran Hirzy

▲ *How to Help Your Board Govern More and Manage Less* by Richard P. Chait

▲ *Hiring the Chief Executive* by Sheila Albert

▲ *Beyond Strategic Planning* by Douglas C. Eadie

▲ *Fulfilling the Public Trust* by Peter D. Bell

▲ *Redesigning the Nonprofit Organization* by Gwendolyn Calvert Baker

▲ *Self-Assessment for Nonprofit Governing Boards* by Larry H. Slesinger

▲ *Developing the Nonprofit Board* by Maureen K. Robinson

▲ *Nonprofit Mergers* by David La Piana

▲ *Governing Boards: Their Nature and Nurture* by Cyril O. Houle

▲ *Six Keys to Recruiting, Orienting, and Involving Nonprofit Board Members* by Judith Grummon Nelson

▲ *Building an Effective Board* (audiocassette)

▲ *Board Members and Risk: A Primer on Protection from Liability*

▲ *Establishing Appropriate Compensation for Chief Executives of Nonprofit Organizations*

▲ *What Every Board Member Should Know about America's Nonprofit Sector*

▲ *Stories from the Board Room, Vol. I: Realities and Rewards of Trusteeship*

▲ *Stories from the Board Room, Vol. II: Living with Complexity: The Lincoln Hill Experience*

Nonprofit Governance Series

1. *Ten Basic Responsibilities of Nonprofit Boards* (also available in Spanish and Portuguese)

2. *The Chief Executive's Role in Developing the Nonprofit Board*

3. *Fund Raising and the Nonprofit Board Member*

4. *Board Assessment of the Chief Executive: A Responsibility Essential to Good Governance*

5. *The Nonprofit Board's Role in Reducing Risk: More Than Buying Insurance*

6. *Strategic Planning and the Nonprofit Board*

7. *Board Passages: Three Key Stages in a Nonprofit Board's Life Cycle*

8. *Understanding Nonprofit Financial Statements: A Primer for Board Members*

9. *Creating and Renewing Advisory Boards: Strategies for Success*

10. *Planning Successful Board Retreats: A Guide for Board Members and Chief Executives*

11. *The Role of the Board Chairperson: For Effective Nonprofit Governance*

12. *Bridging the Gap Between Nonprofit and For-Profit Board Members*

13. *Smarter Board Meetings*

14. *Board Assessment of the Organization: How Are We Doing?*

15. *The Board's Role in Public Relations and Communications*

16. *Finding and Retaining Your Next Chief Executive: Making the Transition Work*